AF380071

To Celebrate

Date

THANK YOU FOR COMING.

Let's celebrate!

Guest Name

Wishes & Messages

Email/Phone

Guest Name

Wishes & Messages

Email/Phone

Guest Name

Wishes & Messages

Email/Phone

Guest Name

Wishes & Messages

Email/Phone

Guest Name

____

Wishes & Messages

____

____

____

____

____

Email/Phone _____________________________

Guest Name

Wishes & Messages

Email/Phone

Guest Name

Wishes & Messages

EMAIL/PHONE

Guest Name

Wishes & Messages

Email/Phone

Guest Name

Wishes & Messages

Email/Phone

Guest Name

Wishes & Messages

Email/Phone

Guest Name

Wishes & Messages

Email/Phone

Guest Name

Wishes & Messages

Email/Phone

Guest Name

Wishes & Messages

Email/Phone

Guest Name

Wishes & Messages

Email/Phone

Guest Name
Wishes & Messages
Email/Phone

Guest Name

Wishes & Messages

Email/Phone

Guest Name

Wishes & Messages

Email/Phone

Guest Name
Wishes & Messages
Email/Phone

Guest Name

Wishes & Messages

EMAIL/PHONE

Guest Name

Wishes & Messages

Email/Phone

Guest Name
Wishes & Messages
Email/Phone

Guest Name

Wishes & Messages

Email/Phone

Guest Name

Wishes & Messages

Email/Phone

Guest Name

Wishes & Messages

Email/Phone

Guest Name
Wishes & Messages
Email/Phone

Guest Name

Wishes & Messages

EMAIL/PHONE

Guest Name

Wishes & Messages

Email/Phone

Guest Name
Wishes & Messages
Email/Phone

Guest Name
Wishes & Messages
Email/Phone

Guest Name

Wishes & Messages

Email/Phone

Guest Name
Wishes & Messages
Email/Phone

Guest Name
Wishes & Messages
Email/Phone

Guest Name

Wishes & Messages

EMAIL/PHONE

Guest Name

Wishes & Messages

Email/Phone

Guest Name
Wishes & Messages
Email/Phone

Guest Name
Wishes & Messages
Email/Phone

Guest Name

Wishes & Messages

EMAIL/PHONE

Guest Name
Wishes & Messages
Email/Phone

Guest Name

Wishes & Messages

Email/Phone

Guest Name

Wishes & Messages

Email/Phone

Guest Name
Wishes & Messages
Email/Phone

Guest Name
Wishes & Messages
Email/Phone

Guest Name
Wishes & Messages
Email/Phone

Guest Name
Wishes & Messages
Email/Phone

Guest Name

Wishes & Messages

Email/Phone

Guest Name

Wishes & Messages

Email/Phone

Guest Name

Wishes & Messages

Email/Phone

Guest Name
Wishes & Messages
EMAIL/PHONE

Guest Name
Wishes & Messages
Email/Phone

Guest Name

Wishes & Messages

Email/Phone

Guest Name
Wishes & Messages
Email/Phone

Guest Name
Wishes & Messages
EMAIL/PHONE

Guest Name

Wishes & Messages

Email/Phone

Guest Name

Wishes & Messages

Email/Phone

Guest Name

Wishes & Messages

Email/Phone

Guest Name

Wishes & Messages

EMAIL/PHONE

Guest Name

Wishes & Messages

Email/Phone

Guest Name

Wishes & Messages

E
EMAIL/PHONE

Guest Name

Wishes & Messages

Email/Phone

Guest Name

Wishes & Messages

EMAIL/PHONE

Guest Name

____

Wishes & Messages

____

____

____

____

____

____

Email/Phone _______________________

Guest Name
Wishes & Messages
Email/Phone

Guest Name

Wishes & Messages

Email/Phone

Guest Name
Wishes & Messages
Email/Phone

Guest Name

Wishes & Messages

Email/Phone

Guest Name

Wishes & Messages

EMAIL/PHONE

Guest Name

Wishes & Messages

Email/Phone

Guest Name

Wishes & Messages

EMAIL/PHONE

Guest Name

Wishes & Messages

Email/Phone

Guest Name

Wishes & Messages

Email/Phone

Guest Name
Wishes & Messages
Email/Phone

Guest Name
Wishes & Messages
Email/Phone

Guest Name

Wishes & Messages

Email/Phone

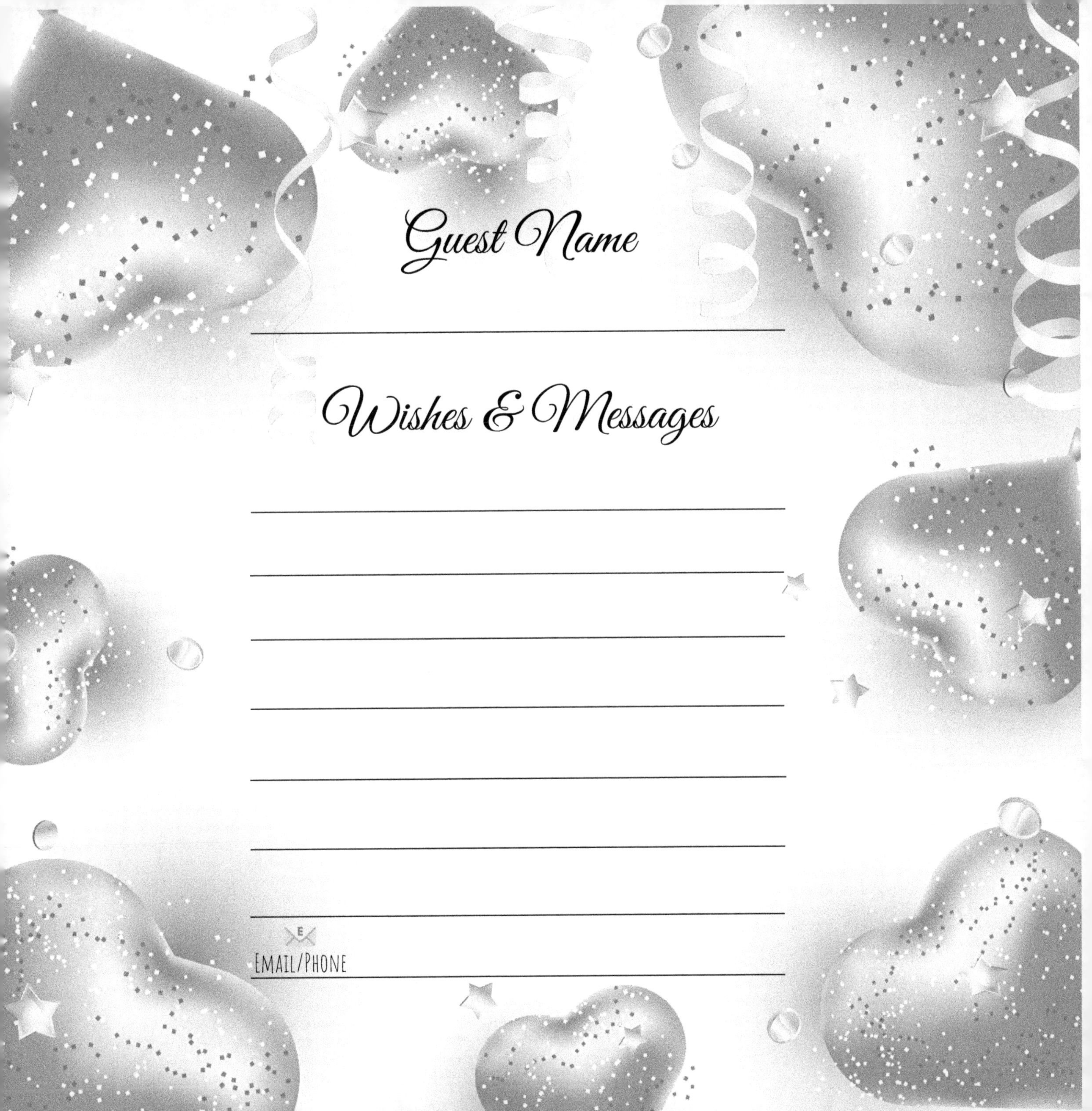

Guest Name

Wishes & Messages

Email/Phone

Guest Name
Wishes & Messages
Email/Phone

Guest Name

Wishes & Messages

EMAIL/PHONE

Guest Name

Wishes & Messages

Email/Phone

Guest Name
Wishes & Messages
EMAIL/PHONE

Guest Name
Wishes & Messages
Email/Phone

Guest Name

Wishes & Messages

EMAIL/PHONE

Guest Name

Wishes & Messages

Email/Phone

Guest Name

Wishes & Messages

Email/Phone

Guest Name
Wishes & Messages
Email/Phone

Guest Name

Wishes & Messages

Email/Phone

Guest Name

Wishes & Messages

Email/Phone

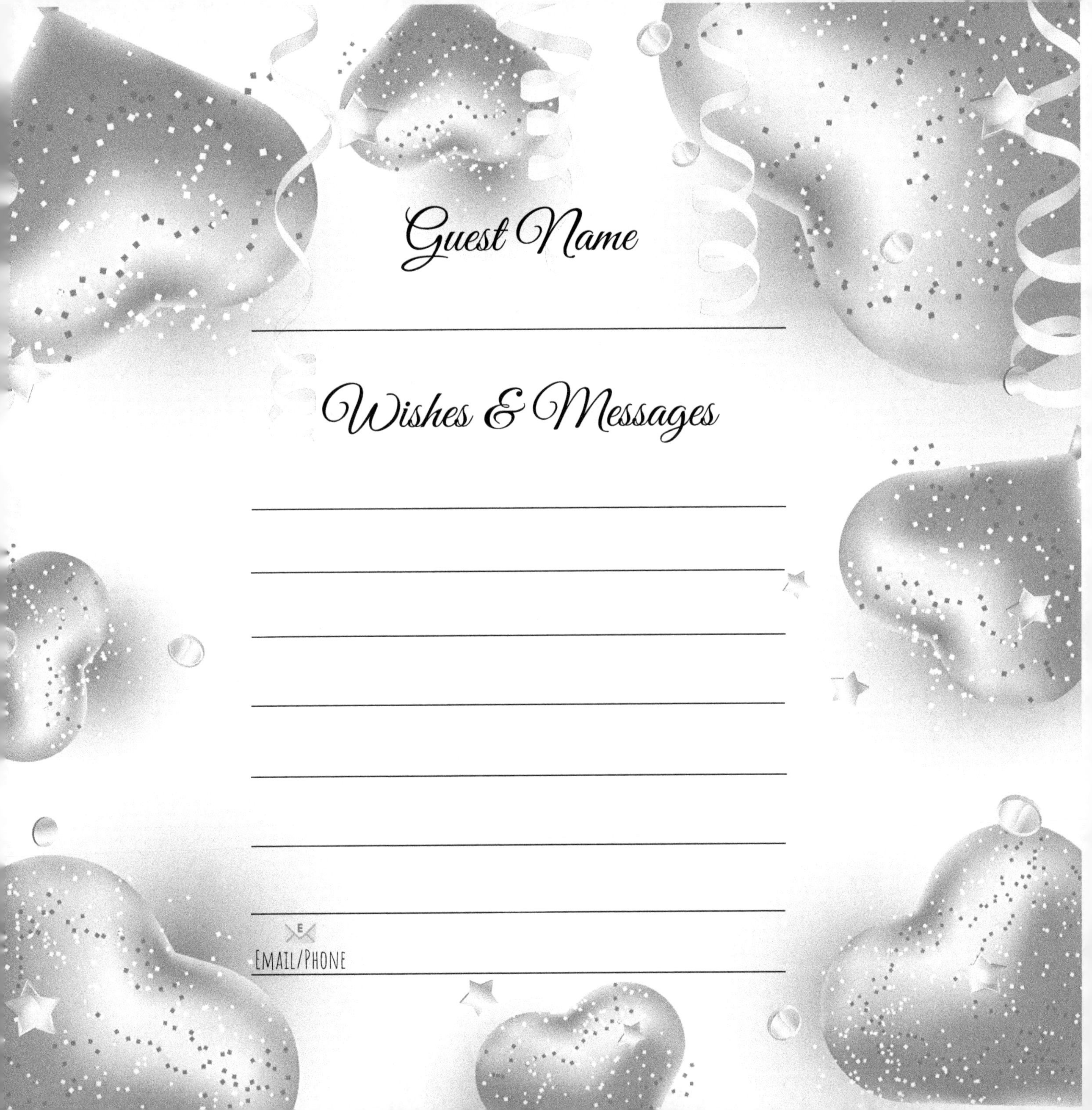

Guest Name

Wishes & Messages

Email/Phone

# Guest Name

Wishes & Messages

Guest Name

Wishes & Messages

EMAIL/PHONE

Guest Name

Wishes & Messages

Email/Phone

Guest Name

Wishes & Messages

Email/Phone

Guest Name

Wishes & Messages

Email/Phone

Guest Name

Wishes & Messages

EMAIL/PHONE

Guest Name
Wishes & Messages
Email/Phone

Guest Name

Wishes & Messages

Email/Phone

Guest Name

Wishes & Messages

E
EMAIL/PHONE

Guest Name

Wishes & Messages

EMAIL/PHONE

Guest Name

Wishes & Messages

Email/Phone

Guest Name

Wishes & Messages

Email/Phone

Guest Name

Wishes & Messages

Email/Phone

Guest Name

Wishes & Messages

EMAIL/PHONE

Guest Name

Wishes & Messages

Email/Phone

Guest Name

Wishes & Messages

EMAIL/PHONE

Guest Name

Wishes & Messages

EMAIL/PHONE

Guest Name
Wishes & Messages
EMAIL/PHONE

Guest Name
Wishes & Messages
Email/Phone

NOTES & PHOTOS

NOTES & PHOTOS

NOTES & PHOTOS

NOTES & PHOTOS

NOTES & PHOTOS

GIFT LOG

Name / Email / Phone | Gift

GIFT LOG

Name /Email /Phone	Gift

GIFT LOG

Name / Email / Phone   Gift

GIFT LOG

<table>
<tr><th>Name /Email /Phone</th><th>Gift</th></tr>
</table>

GIFT LOG

Name /Email /Phone	Gift

GIFT LOG

<table>
<tr><td>*Name /Email /Phone*</td><td>*Gift*</td></tr>
</table>

GIFT LOG

Name / Email / Phone	Gift